SERMON OUTLINES

OUTLINES

FOR

SPECIAL

OCCASIONS

Books by Al Bryant

Climbing the Heights
Day by Day with C. H. Spurgeon
More Sermon Outlines for Special Occasions
More Sermon Outlines on Prayer
New Every Morning
Revival Sermon Outlines
Sermon Outlines for Evangelistic Occasions
Sermon Outlines for Funerals and Other Special Occasions
Sermon Outlines for Lay Leaders
Sermon Outlines on Bible Characters (Old Testament)
Sermon Outlines on Bible Characters (New Testament)
Sermon Outlines on the Attributes of God
Sermon Outlines on the Deeper Life
Sermon Outlines on the Cross of Christ
Sermon Outlines on the Life of Christ
Sermon Outlines on Prayer
Sermon Outlines on Prophetic Themes
Sermon Outlines for Special Occasions
Sermon Outlines for Worship Services
Sourcebook of Poetry

MORE SERMON OUTLINES
FOR
SPECIAL OCCASIONS

compiled by
Al Bryant

kregel
PUBLICATIONS

Grand Rapids, MI 49501

More Sermon Outlines for Special Occasions by Al Bryant.

Copyright © 1995 by Kregel Publications, a division of Kregel, Inc., P. O. Box 2607, Grand Rapids, MI 49501. Kregel Publications provides trusted, biblical publications for Christian growth and service. Your comments and suggestions are valued.

Cover and Book Design: Alan G. Hartman

Library of Congress Cataloging-in-Publication Data
Bryant, Al (1926–
    More sermon outlines for special occasions / [compiled by] Al Bryant.
        p. cm.
    1. Occasional sermons—Outlines, syllabi, etc.
I. Bryant, Al, 1926–
BV4254.2.S45   1995   252'.02—dc20   95-7832
                                                                      CIP

ISBN 0-8254-2268-x (paperback)

          1 2 3 4 5 Printing / Year 99 98 97 96 95

Printed in the United States of America

CONTENTS

Installations

Weddings

Stewardship

Special Occasions

PREFACE

From time to time, every pastor or lay speaker is called upon to bring a Bible-centered message at an unusual occasion—a message that demands extra insight as well as special preparation and deep thought. It is in such situations that you will find this collection of sermon outlines especially helpful and appropriate.

You will find outlines for such special occasions as weddings, baccalaureate services, installations, dedications and other unique situations. However, the outlines will have to be adapted to a special occasion. You will have to exercise your own imagination and ingenuity in reworking the outlines to fit your particular need. For example, some of the outlines included in the "Graduation" section will seem, at first glance, somewhat irrelevant. But upon careful reflection you will discover a message that will fit the background of the occasion with a minimum of adaptation and revamping.

These outlines are intended as "pump primers" and "sermon starters," not as "crutches." They are "springboards," but the "swimming" is up to you. If they perform that task, the work of the compiler will have been worthwhile.

AL BRYANT

SCRIPTURE INDEX

GOD'S WAY

Shew me thy ways, O Lord; teach me thy paths (Ps. 25:4).

What a magnificent verse for facing life! What a motto for one who wants to serve the Lord. What a guide for going God's way:

1. **Its Characteristics**
   A way of truth (Ps. 25:5)
   A way of mercy (Ps. 25:10)
   A way of obedience (Ps. 69:32)
   A way of peace (Prov. 3:17)
   A way of holiness (Isa. 35:8)
   A way of safety (Isa. 35:9)
   A way of prosperity (Gen. 24:56)

2. **Natural Man Ignorant—Must Be Taught**
   "Teach me" (Ps. 27:11)
   "Show me" (Ps. 25:4)
   "Lead me" (Ps. 25:5)

3. **Who May Know God's Way?**
   The meek (1 Peter 5:5)
   The obedient (John 7:17)
   The man of faith (Acts 3:16; John 3:16)

4. **How May He Learn?**
   Through Christ (John 6:40; John 8:12; John 10:28; John 10:9)

Sermons in a Nutshell

THE CHRISTIAN'S RACE

Hebrews 12:1–2

I. **The Personalities at the Race**—"A cloud of witnesses"

II. **The Preparation for the Race**—"Lay aside every weight"

III. **The Persistence in the Race**—"Run with patience"

IV. **The Purpose of the Race**—"Looking unto Jesus"

C. M. Ward

WORKING FOR GOD

EXHORTATION for the work	"Go"	(Matt. 21:28)
SPHERE for the work	"My Vineyard"	(Matt. 21:28)
SEASON for the work	"Today"	(Matt. 21:28)
POWER for the work	"Holy Ghost"	(Acts 1:8)
RESULT of the work	"Added," etc.	(Acts 2:41)
REWARD for the work	"Shall shine"	(Dan. 12:3)

Pegs for Preachers

WHAT HAVE YOU?

What is that in thine hand? (Ex. 4:2)

1. Moses Had a Rod, and it became a wand.

2. David Had a Sling, and used it to slay a giant.

3. A Jewish Maid Had a Little Voice, and used it to tell of the man of God (Naaman . . . Elisha).

4. A Little Lad Had His Lunch, and Jesus used it to feed a multitude.

5. A Widow Had Two Mites, but millions have been inspired by her giving.

6. Dorcas Had Only a Sewing Kit, but used it in a big way to help the poor.

"What is that in thine hand?"

Sermon Starters, P. E. Holdcraft

THE CALLING OF THE CHILD OF GOD

2 Timothy 1:9

1. We Are Called Out of Darkness (1 Peter 2:9).
Our experiences when born again, and we came into light (Eph. 5:11–14; 1 Thess. 5:4–5).

2. We Are Called to Sonship (1 John 3:1–2).
We were at one time outside of the heavenly family (John 1:12; Phil. 2:15).

3. We Are Called to Fellowship (1 Cor. 1:9).
With the Father, the Son and believers in Christ (Acts 2:42; 1 John 1:3, 7).

4. We Are Called to Liberty (Gal. 5:13).
Free men in Christ and no longer under bondage (Rom. 6:17–18; 8:21; 2 Cor. 3:17).

5. We Are Called to Peace (Col. 3:15).
The natural, normal condition for a believer (Rom. 5:1; Eph. 2:14–15).

6. We Are Called to Blessings (1 Peter 3:9).
Blessings are ours—do we possess our possessions (Rom. 15:29; Eph. 1:3)?

7. We Are Called to Glory (1 Peter 5:10).
We anticipate the prospect which is before us (John 17:24; 1 Thess. 2:12).

C. C. Maple

WHAT CHRISTIANS SHOULD BE

Well pleasing in his sight (Heb. 13:21)

    I.   Imitators of God—(Eph. 5:1)
   II.   Blameless—(Eph. 1:4; 1 Peter 1:14–16)
  III.   Transformed—(Rom. 12:2)
  IV.   Separated—(2 Cor. 6:17)
   V.   Examples—(1 Tim. 4:12)
  VI.   Fruitful—(Rom. 7:4)
 VII.   Thankful—(Col. 3:15; Eph. 5:20)
VIII.   Contented—(Heb. 13:5)

Treasures of Bible Truth

THE SERVANT IS TO—

Walk .... 1 Thessalonians 4:12

Watch .... 1 Thessalonians 5:6

Wait .... 1 Thessalonians 1:10

Witness........... 1 Thessalonians 1:7

Warn .... 1 Thessalonians 5:14

Work .... 1 Thessalonians 1:3

Pegs for Preachers

THREEFOLD WORK OF CHRIST

Titus 2

1. **Work of Grace** .... verse 11 ...... Past

2. **Work of Godliness** ..... verse 12 ...... Present

3. **Work of Glory** .... verse 13 ...... Future

1,000 Sermon Outlines, T. W. Callaway

THE WORD OF GOD

Thy word have I hid in mine heart,
that I might not sin against thee (Ps. 119:11).

   I. Lives—1 Peter 1:23
  II. Abides—1 John 2:14
 III. Pierces—Hebrews 4:12
 IV. Sanctifies—1 Timothy 4:4, 5
  V. Discerns—Hebrews 4:12
 VI. Works—1 Thessalonians 2:13
VII. Prevails—Acts 19:20

Treasures of Bible Truth

EIGHT POINTS FOR WORKERS

1. **Strong**. "Be strong in the grace"   2 Timothy 2:1
2. **Endure**. "Endure hardness"   2 Timothy 2:3
3. **Study**. "Study to show thyself approved"   2 Timothy 2:15
4. **Shun**. "Shun profane and vain babblings"   2 Timothy 2:16
5. **Flee**. "Flee also youthful lusts"   2 Timothy 2:22
6. **Avoid**. "Foolish and unlearned
   questions avoid"   2 Timothy 2:23
7. **Patient**. "The servant . . . patient"   2 Timothy 2:24
8. **Follow**. "Follow righteousness," etc.   2 Timothy 2:22

Bible Themes for Busy Workers

GROWTH IN GRACE

Grow in grace (2 Peter 3:18)

I. False Marks of Growth in Grace
   A. Increasing religious knowledge.
   B. Pleasure in conversing on religious topics.
   C. Pleasure in hearing the Word.
   D. Zeal for the cause of religion.
II. The True Marks of Growth in Grace
   A. An increasing humility.
   B. A self-denying spirit.
   C. Simplicity and innocence of mind.
   D. Increasing hatred of falsehood and artifice.
III. The Means to Be Used
   A. Secret prayer.
   B. A diligent perusal of the Word.
   C. Careful self-examination.

The Pulpit Synopsis

THE MISSION OF THE CHURCH

Acts 1:8

I. **The Mission Is to Preach and Teach the Word** (2 Tim. 4:2).

A. We can look to no one else to do this work (Matt. 28:19–20; Acts 4:31; 8:4).

B. The Early Church did not seek to entertain (Acts 6:4).

II. **The Mission Is to Provide a House of Prayer** (Isa. 56:7).

A. God's people have always been a people of prayer (Acts 1:14; 6:4; Col. 4:2).

B. By prayer, solution to problems, unity, etc. (Acts 4:24).

III. **The Mission Is to Sustain Divine Worship** (Acts 2:42).

A. Important for spiritual life, especially young converts (Mal. 3:16–17; Acts 20:7; Heb. 10:25).

B. Congregations were established, elders ordained, and churches set in order (Acts 15:36).

IV. **The Mission Is to Defend the Christian Faith** (Jude 3).

A. Danger from within as well as from without (1 Cor. 1:12–13; 2:2; 2 Tim. 3:1).

B. Unless we know the faith we cannot defend it (2 Tim. 4:7).

V. **The Mission Is to Make Known the Gospel to the World** (Mark 16:15–16).

A. Any "Good Samaritan" on any "Jericho Road" is commissioned (Luke 24:47–48; Acts 1:8; Rom. 1:14–17).

B. Through visiting to the nations (Acts 15:14) the church is built (8:4).

VI. **The Mission Is to Edify and Build Up the Church** (Acts 20:28).

A. Individual members are likened unto babes (Eph. 4:14; Col. 2:6–7; 1 Peter 2:2).

B. Why so many "weak" and "feeble" Christians? (Acts 9:31).

VII. The Mission Is to Proclaim the Lord's Return (Titus 2:13, 15).
A. If you "love" His appearing—you will talk of it (1 Thess. 2:19; 2 Tim. 4:8; Heb. 9:28).
B. It was preached by the Early Church (James 5:8).

C. C. Maple

SEVEN POSSIBILITIES OF A STRONG CHURCH

Philippians 4:13

1. A Strong Church Will Be Able to Stand (Eph. 6:10–11).
We are in a fight—it takes strength to stand (Eph. 6:13–14; 1 Peter 5:10).

2. A Strong Church Will Be a Testimony (Titus 2:1–2, 7–8).
Individual influence—church influence (1 Tim. 4:12, 16; Titus 2:11–14).

3. A Strong Church Will Glorify God (Eph. 3:16–21).
The members will reflect the glory of God (Acts 2:47; 4:13).

4. A Strong Church Will Be Able to Help Others (Rom. 15:1).
Help—financial, moral, spiritual (Gal. 6:2; James 2:14–18).

5. A Strong Church Will Be an Example to All (1 Tim. 1:16).
Example is a pattern, or a "model to be copied" (2 Cor. 3:2; 1 Thess. 1:3, 8).

6. A Strong Church Will Be Able to Accomplish Much (Phil. 4:13).
The members will be able to get the Gospel out (Acts 4:33; 8:4; Rom. 10:17–18).

7. A Strong Church Will Be Found Ready to Meet the Lord (Matt. 25:10).
The members will be living in daily expectation (Luke 12:34–38; Heb. 9:28).

C. C. Maple

THE CHURCHES OF CHRIST

Romans 16:16

I. The Proper Origin, or Beginning
A. Christ is both Founder and Foundation.

B. He has used, and still uses certain people, Spirit-filled, to plant and to build.

II. This Church an Organism
A. This means "A living body fitted to carry on life action."

B. The church of Christ begets and produces "babes in Christ," a living family.

III. This Organism a Spiritually Functioning Organization
A. A living human body made up of various members all working together harmoniously, fulfilling the purpose for which it was placed in the body, is the Bible illustration of the organized church.

B. Various gifts of the Spirit are given to the members to qualify them for the variety of needs and operations within the church of Christ.

IV. The Place of Baptism and the Lord's Supper in the Churches of Christ
"I praise you, that ye keep the ordinances, as I delivered them to you" (1 Cor. 11:2). These were kept in accord with the purpose for which they were delivered:

A. The right objective.

B. The right order.

C. A regular, reverent, observing of them.

V. The New Testament Pattern Concerning Officers and Offerings
A. Officers (see Acts 1:21–26; 6:1–6).

B. Offerings (see Gen. 14:20; Matt. 23:23; 1 Cor. 16:1–2).

VI. Obligation of a Church of Christ to Evangelize, Baptize and Catechize

VII. Optimistic Outlook to Be Maintained by a Church of Christ
(See Acts 1:11 and 1 Thess. 4:13–18).

adapted from *John A. Ross*

THE PEOPLE HAD A MIND TO WORK

Nehemiah 4:6

Introduction
Great causes have always challenged men.
Some people respond to small causes.
Some respond only to great causes.
Some respond to no cause until they see how it affects them.
Some illustrations: Remember the Alamo; remember the "Maine"; remember Pearl Harbor.

I. **Christ Saw the People as Sheep without a Shepherd and Had Compassion on Them**

II. **We Are Moved by Civic Needs**
    A. Community Chest, Red Cross and disaster needs.
    B. We are moved by material needs—public highways, bridges and other needs.
    C. We are moved by spiritual needs—church buildings, revivals and religious training.

III. **Cooperation Is Necessary**
    A. Hundreds worked together to save little Kathy Fiscus, entombed in a well.
    B. All government units need close cooperation to function properly.
    C. We, as sons of God, spiritual brothers, need to work side by side to save a lost world. Pray, plan and labor together with God.

IV. **There Are Four Essentials for Successful Building**
    A. A proper perspective.
    B. Ability to utilize existing materials.
    C. The consideration or final use of all our efforts. The motive for building.
    D. The harnessing of all resources and complete dedication of ourselves and materials to the achievement of our greatest goal, which is the salvation of the lost.

A. F. Raloff

The ideal church as revealed in the New Testament, like the New Jerusalem, has twelve gates.

1. **The Foundation of the Church:** the kingship of Jesus. "Thou art the Christ. . . . Upon this rock will I build my church" (Matt. 16:18).

2. **The Atoning Price of the Church:** the blood of Christ. "The church . . . which he purchased with his own blood" (Acts 20:28).

3. **The Administrator of the Church:** the Holy Spirit. He sets "in the church" His gifts, severally as He will (1 Cor. 12:28).

4. **The Head of the Church:** the ascended Lord (Eph. 1:23; 5:23).

5. **The Motive and Moving Power of the Church:** love. The members are to love each other "as Christ loved the church" (Eph. 5:2, 5, 25).

6. **The Life of the Church:** prayer, the power that brings release, even as it did to imprisoned Peter, when prayer was "made without ceasing of the church unto God" (Acts 12:5).

7. **The Privilege of the Church:** worship of the Lord. Christ is ever the One who in the midst of the church leads her in praise to God (Heb. 2:12); and the church is responsible, as well as privileged, to "come together" to remember the Lord's death (1 Cor. 11:18–26).

8. **The Rule of the Church:** edification, or building each other up (1 Cor. 14:5, 12, 19).

9. **The Responsibility of the Church:** unity of action. There are to be no schisms in the body, but each member is to tarry for one another, and hold the Head by recognizing the members in mutual helps and assemblage (Eph. 2:18–22; 4:16).

10. **The Custody of the Church:** the truth. The church of God is the pillar and ground of the truth (1 Tim. 3:15).

11. **The Center and Circumference of the Church:** God. It is called "the church of God," "the church in God the Father, and the Lord Jesus Christ," "the church of the first-born" (1 Cor 1:2; 1 Thess. 1:1; Heb. 12:23).

12. **The End of the Church:** the glory of God. It displays His manifest wisdom and is to be to His manifested glory (Eph. 3:10, 21; 5:27).

adapted from *F. E. Marsh*

DECLARING OUR ALLEGIANCE

Exodus 32:26

Introduction
An amazing scene in the camp of the Israelites.
People miraculously guided by God.
Same people now want guidance of dumb idol.
The question: "Who is on the Lord's side?"

I. **Those Who Were Opposed**
   A. The majority remained in the camp.
   B. They preferred a "god" of their own creation.

II. **Those Who Were Indifferently Disposed**
   A. They served a god of expedience—the mixed multitude.
   B. The neutralist is a menace to any organization.
   C. If we don't position ourselves—then we automatically line up against God.

III. **Those Who Were Emphatically Posed**
   A. They made a definite decision for God.
   B. They took subsequent action by separation from sin.
   C. They obeyed the commandments given.
   D. They demonstrated an interest in spiritual things.

E. S. Phillips

THE CHURCH'S ONE FOUNDATION

1 Corinthians 3:11

Introduction

A foundation is the groundwork or lowest part of a building, which supports the other parts; as the foundation of a house, of a castle, of a fort, tower, etc. Christ is called a foundation (Isa. 28:16). On Him, as the foundation, the church is built.

I. The Necessity of This Foundation

It is necessary because:

A. *Man is a sinner.* He is a transgressor, lost and hopeless. His heart is impure. God is against him. Divine justice condemns him.

B. *He is helpless.* He is "without strength" (Rom. 5:6). He is totally incapable of removing or avoiding the awful penalty.

II. The Properties of This Foundation

A. *Its origin is divine.*

B. A foundation must have *strength* and *stability* in order to support the superstructure.

C. Christ is a *precious foundation.*

D. Christ is a *tried foundation.*

E. Christ is an *everlasting foundation.*

III. The Duty and Privilege of Believers to Build, or Rest upon This Foundation

This implies:

A. Credence, a belief that He is appointed of God to be the foundation—the Savior.

B. A conviction that this foundation is necessary.

C. The abandonment of all other grounds of trust.

D. Dependence upon Him. Even as a stone is placed upon the foundation, so must we place our souls upon Christ the Rock.

Selected

Who Is Dead?

A preacher who found no one at prayer meeting began to toll the bell. A dozen folks came running in, and one asked, "Who is dead?"

"The church," replied the preacher as he pulled away at the rope.

Selected

THE SECURITY OF THE CHURCH

Matthew 7:25

Introduction

The comparison of the Great Teacher in the context indicates the safety and happiness of those who trust in Christ, and the misery of those who reject Him. The language is also calculated to afford encouragement and hope. Sometimes Zion is opposed, afflicted, and clouded, and then her people mourn and tremble for the future. But Zion is founded upon a rock, and cannot be shaken.

I. The Character of the Church of Christ

The character of God's people is described in verse 24, "Whosoever heareth," etc.

A. *They are wise.* Like the man who built his house upon a rock. This procedure denotes wisdom, foresight and precaution.

B. *They revere the truth.* "Hear these sayings of mine." They do not lean to their own understandings, but regard Christ as a wise and infallible Teacher.

C. *They do His will.* "Heareth these sayings of mine, *and doeth them.*" This is more than mere profession.

II. The Ground of Their Confidence

"It was founded upon a rock." Christ is called "that Rock" (1 Cor. 10:4). His finished work on the Cross as the great atoning sacrifice is the foundation of the Christian's faith and hope. And it is firmer than a rock. See Isaiah 28:16. "A rock" conveys the idea:

A. *Of strength and power.*

B. *Of durability.* Christ is called the Rock of Ages, and is subject to no change. He is immutable. He is the "same yesterday," etc.

III. The Security of the Church in the Time of Trial

"It fell not." This implies:

A. *That the church is frequently assailed by opposition.* Its strength and durability must be tried.

B. *That the church has withstood all opposition.* "It fell not." While other systems have fallen, and are almost forgotten, the church continues firmly fixed on the immutable Savior.

Sometimes, like Israel, it multiplies under oppression. Frequently the blood of the martyrs has been the seed of the church.

Behold the antediluvian church in the family of Noah, outriding the flood itself. "It fell not."

Behold the Jewish church preserved in Babylon, and amidst the mighty convulsions that followed, more durable than the conquests of Alexander. "It fell not."

Behold the Christian church, outliving even the eternal Rome; and, sheltered amidst the barbarism of the middle ages, her light burst the cloud at the glorious Reformation, a light which has ever since been prevailing against the darkness of error, and subduing men to its influence. "It fell not."

Walk then about Zion, mark her bulwarks, consider her palaces, and from the past we may take up this triumphant strain, "This God is our God forever and ever."

Application

Let this subject dispel despondency as to the issue of God's Church.

How safe are believers! They are upon "the Rock."

Selected

THE EARLY CHURCH

The members of the Early Church were characterized by:

1. Their *Constancy*.   "Continued," Acts 2:42.

2. Their *Energy*.   "Daily," Acts 2:46.

3. Their *Unity*.   "One accord," Acts 2:46.

4. Their *Liberality*.   "Sold their possessions," Acts 2:45.

5. Their *Simplicity*. "Had all things common," Acts 2:44.

6. Their *Charity*.   "From house to house," Acts 2:46.

7. Their *Fidelity*. "Steadfastly in the apostles' doctrine," Acts 2:42.

8. Their *Sincerity*.   "Singleness of heart," Acts 2:46.

Charles Inglis

GOD AND GOD'S CHURCH

I. The Beginning of God's Church (Acts 2:41–47)
  A. Began with indispensable salvation (v. 41).
  B. Began with indispensable spiritual development (v. 42).
  C. Began with divine power (v. 43).
  D. Began with God-honoring love (v. 44).
  E. Began with God-imparted sacrifice and God-wrought provision (v. 45).
  F. Began with public worship of God, public testimony to God, heavenly gladness, and with desire for God's glory (v. 46).
  G. Began with praise to God, effective impression upon mankind, God-wrought growth and God's endorsement (v. 47).
  H. Began with God-energized fellowship (vv. 41–47).

II. The Development of God's Church (Eph. 4:11–16)
  A. The means of the church's development (v. 11).
  B. The evidence of the church's development (v. 12).
  C. The period of the church's development (v. 13).
  D. The climax (goal) of its development (v. 13).
  E. The safeguard through development (v. 14).
  F. The blessedness of development (v. 15).
  G. The process in development (v. 16).
  H. The result of the church's development (v. 16).

William McCarrell

GOD'S PEOPLE

But ye are a peculiar people (1 Peter 2:9)

  I. God's People Are a Professing People
  II. God's People Are a Separated People
  III. God's People Are a Suffering People
  IV. God's People Are a Praying People
  V. God's People Are a Sanctified People
  VI. God's People Are a Blessed People

Pulpit Germs, W. W. Wythe

IN THE CHURCH WE PREACH CHRIST

1 Corinthians 1:23

1. **We Preach That Jesus Is the Lord** (Rom. 10:9).
He is exalted to be both Lord and Christ (Matt. 16:16; John 1:45, 49; Acts 2:36).

2. **We Preach That Christ Is the Savior from Sin** (Matt. 1:21).
Salvation is through Him alone (Luke 24:47; Acts 4:10–12; 5:31).

3. **We Preach Christ as the Only Source of Life** (John 3:16).
The First Adam brought death—the second Adam brought life (John 1:4; 3:36; 1 Cor. 15:22; Col. 3:3–4).

4. **We Preach Christ as the Christian's Guide** (John 10:3).
As Moses and Joshua were guides to Israel so Christ is our guide (Pss. 23; 73:24; Isa. 40:11; John 10:3).

5. **We Preach Christ as Our Great Example** (1 Peter 2:21).
Follow Him (not a stranger). Know His voice (Matt. 16:24; 1 Cor. 11:1; 1 John 2:6).

6. **We Preach Christ as Our Intercessor** (Heb. 7:25).
Access to the Father is only through Him (Luke 22:31–32; John 16:23–24).

7. **We Preach Christ as the Believer's Hope** (1 Thess. 2:19).
Without Him there is no hope beyond (John 14:3; Phil. 3:20–21; Titus 2:13).

C. C. Maple

On God's Side
Someone once asked Abraham Lincoln to appoint a day of prayer and fasting that God might be on their side. "Don't bother about that," said the President, "God is now on the right side; you get with Him."

W. E. Daniels

THE WORK OF THE LORD IN THE CHURCH

Psalm 126:3

Every heart should meditate daily on the marvelous works of the Lord, and especially what He has done for every one of us.

1. The Lord Gives Life.

All life is from the Lord. He alone is able to give. He is the source of life. We live and move and have our being in Him. He is anxious that life shall be abundant, glorious and gracious. We accept His gift of life.

2. The Lord Sustains Life.

The Lord does not hurl life on us and then go away to leave us alone. He gives life and then remains with us always to encourage and to sustain and to support.

3. The Lord Reveals Himself to Us.

Until the fullness of His revelation came in Christ, the Lord revealed Himself to men as rapidly as they were able to comprehend. He revealed Himself through His spirit, His angels, seers, prophets, priests, and finally in fullness through His only begotten Son, the Lord Jesus Christ, and the Holy Spirit. Gracious is the Lord.

4. The Lord Gave the Book.

The Lord has given us a marvelous record of His revelation and His work in the Bible. He directed the writing of this great Book and has preserved it and protected and promoted it through the ages. We have His Word in our own language, in many versions, and may read and study it when and where we desire. What a privilege to have His mighty message!

5. The Lord Saves the Soul.

Through the death of Christ on the Cross, the Father has provided the way of eternal life for every soul that will accept it. It is by the grace of God through faith that the soul may come to possess everlasting life. No other gift can compare with this. No other blessing is greater. Surely the Lord does great things for us.

6. The Lord Uses Believers

It is one of the greatest joys of the Christian to be permitted of the Lord to be a co-laborer with Him. He calls consecrated believers along by His side to work with Him in proclaiming the Gospel, promoting the kingdom, and pointing people to the upward way of life.

The Lord has done great things for us. He is doing great things for us now. He will do even greater things for us in the future if we will continue to follow Him.

J. O. Williams

THE TRAGEDY OF A STAGNANT VISION

Proverbs 29:18

Introduction:
Lift up your eyes.

I. Evidences of Stagnation
A. Fields are white and laborers are few.
B. Houses of pleasure are full, churches are partly empty.
C. Growth of delinquency and moral laxness.
D. Sin in the saddle and the world in confusion.

II. Dangers of Stagnation
A. Decay and destruction of principles, ideals.
B. Loss of freedom, personal and national.
C. Internal weakness and inertia.
D. Loss of hope, will to advance, and desire to resist wrong.

III. A Great Challenge That Faces the Church
A. "Where there is no vision, the people perish."
B. We must accept personal responsibility for preserving righteousness and all good.
C. We must keep hope alive in the world.

IV. Steps to Understanding
A. World conditions, tragedies and increasing sinfulness help us to understand the present need.
B. The brevity of time and the certainty of judgment all cause us to be alert.
C. The voice of the prophet must be heard above the din of confusion now so evident in the world.

A. F. Raloff

CHRIST'S PLAN FOR HIS CHURCH

Ephesians 5:25–27

Introduction

People today seem to believe that there is no real program for Christian living. As long as you belong to some church and do your best, everything is all right. This sermon seeks to portray Christ's plan for His church. Christ gave Himself for His church:

I. That He Might Sanctify and Cleanse It

A. Christ gave His all for the church.

B. Christ expects His followers to go all the way with Him.

II. That He Might Present It to Himself a Glorious Church

A. The church needs cleansing to be glorious.

B. The church must be perfect, "without spot . . ."

III. That It Should Be Holy and without Blemish

A. The nature of Christ demands holiness.

B. The sacrifice of Christ expects holiness.

Conclusion

If every member of Christ's church were like me, would it be without spot, and could it be called holy? He has made provision; we must enter into it.

Jack Pischel

—The mightiest man who ever lived could not deliver himself from his sins. If a man could have saved himself, Christ would never have come into the world.

—He came to deliver us from our sinful dispositions, and create in us pure hearts, and when we have Him with us it will not be hard for us. Then the service of Christ will be delightful.

D. L. Moody

THE CHURCH UNDER GOD'S SHELTER

Isaiah 32:2

1. God Provides a Refuge in the Ark—(Gen. 7:1).
When there was no way—He made a way (Rom. 5:6; Acts 4:12).

2. God Provides Protection Under the Blood (Ex. 12:13).
There is only one provision—no substitute (Mark 16:15–16; Heb. 9:22, 26).

3. God Provides Shelter Under the Cloud (Ex. 14:20).
Guidance through the land of the enemy (Ps. 73:24; Heb. 13:5–6).

4. God Provides a Hiding Place—A Refuge (Num. 35:13).
It was necessary that they enter the city (Ps. 46:1, 7, 11; Isa. 26:20).

5. God Provides Salvation Through His Cross (John 3:14–16).
Old Testament types find their fulfillment here (Rom. 1:16; 1 Cor. 1:23).

6. God Provides a Keeping Power for His Own (1 Peter 1:5).
Secure as was Israel on Passover night (Ps. 125:1–2; John 10:27–28).

7. God Provides a Cloud of Glory for His Church (1 Thess. 4:17).
Song—"Caught up in the clouds and received into Glory" (John 14:3; 1 Thess. 2:19).

C. C. Maple

Prayer on Entering Church
Heat and burden of the day
Help us, Lord, to put away.
Let no crowding, fretting cares
Keep earth-bound our spirit's prayers.
Carping criticism take
From our hearts for Jesus' sake.

Author Unknown

DEDICATION OF A CHURCH TO GOD

2 Chronicles 7

I. **Dedication of Buildings in Bible Days.**

A. The tabernacle was dedicated (Num. 7).

B. The temple of Solomon was dedicated (1 Kings 8; 2 Chron. 7:5).

C. The second temple was dedicated (Ezra 6:16–17).

D. The new walls of Jerusalem were dedicated (Neh. 12:27).

E. All things to be holy unto God for His service and the worship of His people should be dedicated (1 Chron. 28:12).

II. **Dedication of the Temple (1 Kings 8).**

A. A great crowd assembled (vv. 1, 5).

B. The ark of the Lord was brought up (vv. 1, 6).

C. A feast was held (v. 65).

D. The presence of God was real (vv. 10–11).

E. Solomon preached a sermon (vv. 12–21).

F. Solomon prayed the dedication prayer (vv. 22–53).

III. **Dedication of This House of God.**

A. We dedicate it holy unto God for His glory only.

B. We release our personal claims upon it.

C. We use it as a means to rededicate our hearts and lives.

adapted from *John C. Jernigan*

SEVEN THINGS CHRISTIANS IN THE CHURCH SHOULD DO

They should live—

I. A Life of Holiness (1 Thess. 5:22; 2 Tim. 2:19).

II. A Life of Prayer (1 Tim. 2:8; 1 Thess. 5:17).

III. A Life of Death (Heb. 11:6; Col. 1:23).

IV. A Life of Self-Denial (Matt. 5:29; Gal. 5:24).

V. A Life of Separation from World (Exod. 32:26).

VI. A Life of Consecration (Exod. 28:40–41; Rom. 12:1).

VII. A Life of Service (Deut. 10:12; Luke 16:13).

Seed Basket

IN THE NAME OF THE LORD WILL WE SET UP OUR BANNERS

Psalm 20:5

1. **The Banner of Loyalty to Christ**
   Faithful devotion—loyalty to Christ first (Josh. 1:16; Rom. 12:1–2).

2. **The Banner of Love for the Brethren (1 Peter 1:22)**
   This is the badge of discipleship. Wear it (1 John 3:11, 14; 4:20–21).

3. **The Banner of Right Thinking and Speaking (Phil. 4:8)**
   Think right if you would speak right (Prov. 23:7; Matt. 2:34; 2 Peter 3:11).

4. **The Banner of Christian Living (Titus 2:11–12)**
   Through careless living, influence is destroyed (Rom. 8:12–13; 1 Peter 1:14–18).

5. **The Banner of Good Works (James 2:18)**
   Christ our example went about "doing" (Acts 1:1; Gal. 6:1–6; Phil. 2:12).

6. **The Banner of Separation (2 Cor. 6:17)**
   The natural trend is to follow the crowd (Gen. 5:24; Ps. 1:1–2).

7. **The Banner of Consecration (1 Chron. 29:5)**
   A holy life—dedicated to Christ (Josh. 14:8; 1 Tim. 2:21).

C. C. Maple

Prayer
In this hour of worship
Grant Thy presence, Lord!
Here, the world forgotten,
Feed us on Thy Word.
From our sins and sorrows
Here we seek release;
Of Thy love persuaded,
Find the path of peace.

Author Unknown

TRUE CONSECRATION

Proverbs 23:26

1. Founded in the love of God (Matt. 22:37; 1 John 3:22).

2. Serving God above all things (Rom. 12:1, 11).

3. Living for Christ (2 Cor. 5:15; Gal. 2:20).

4. Giving glory to the Lord (1 Cor. 10:31).

5. Walking worthy of our vocation (Eph. 4:1; 1 Thess. 2:12).

6. Guided by the Spirit (Rom 8:1, 13).

7. Separated from worldly things (Rom. 6:2, 7).

A. B. Carrero

YE BELONG TO CHRIST

I. "Ye are not your own, for ye are bought with a price" (1 Cor. 6:20).
   A. His purchased possession—(Eph. 1:14).
   B. His redeemed—(1 Peter 18:19).
   C. His peculiar treasure—(Mal. 3:17, R.V.).
   D. His temple, of which He is the chief cornerstone—(Eph. 2:20–22).
   E. His Church, of which He is the Head—(Eph. 5:23).

II. Members of His body, and of His flesh and of His bones (Eph. 5:30).

III. Quickened together with Him; raised up together with Him; sealed together with Him (Eph. 2:5, 6).

IV. "Because Ye Belong to Christ."
   A. "Beloved . . . be diligent, that ye may be found in Him in peace, without spot, and blameless"—(2 Peter 3:14).

Twelve Baskets Full

THE FIRM FOUNDATION

1 Corinthians 3:11

This is a day in which due consideration should be given to foundations. Study the nuggets of gold in this passage.

1. The Need of a Foundation

"For other foundation can no man lay." Man needs God to lay the firm foundation. He cannot lay a firm one without God. In this day when many things are flimsy and shallow in the minds of men, we must get back to the foundation laid by the Lord. A firm foundation is necessary for life in time and eternity. We can afford to build life on the Book, character on the Christ, and the community on the church.

2. The Nature of the Foundation

"That is laid." The Lord has laid the necessary Foundation. It is in the Book, the church, and the Christ. It is a spiritual foundation. It is firm. It is eternal. It will not fail in time and eternity. It is worthy of our faith. It deserves our acceptance. If what we do shall stand, it must be on this foundation.

3. The Name of the Foundation

"Which is Jesus Christ." Not concrete, but Christ who is everlasting. Not steel, but Spirit which is eternal. Only the loving Father could give the Christ to be the foundation for all that is good and great in life on earth and life in heaven. He is the firm foundation. Build upon Him. Build with the best spiritual material. Such building will stand the test of storm and time and eternity.

J. O. Williams

Is This Your Church?

A room of quiet, a temple of peace;
The home of faith—where doubtings cease.
A house of comfort, where hope is given;
A source of strength to make earth Heaven;
A shrine of worship, a place to pray—
I found all this in my church today.

Pulpit Digest

I WILL BUILD MY CHURCH

Matthew 16:18

Introduction

These are the words of Jesus Christ Himself. He came to redeem man. He will succeed.

I. The Meaning of the Church

A. Jesus introduced a new concept when He used the word church.

B. He sought to shift the thinking of the disciples *from* the kingdom idea with its worldly implications *to* the Christian ideals and purposes expressed in the word church.

II. The Foundation of the Church (various theories)

A. He will build the church upon Peter—*false*.

B. He will build the church on the ecclesiastical foundations of the church fathers—*a partial truth*.

C. He will build the church upon Himself, Christ and the confession of His followers—*true*.

III. The Order of Growth of the Church

A. Personal experience—only basis of fellowship.

B. Personal witnessing—only means of propagation.

C. Personal experience makes one a part of the building. Personal witnessing makes one a builder of the building.

Fred Reedy

Churches

Beautiful is the large church,
With stately arch and steeple;
Neighborly is the small church,
With groups of friendly people;
Reverent is the old church,
With centuries of grace;
And a wooden church or a stone church
Can hold an altar place.
And whether it be a rich church
Or a poor church anywhere,
Truly it is a great church
If God is worshiped there.

Author Unknown

CHRISTIANS IN THE EARLY CHURCH

Acts 2:42

1. They Were Grounded in Christian Doctrine (Acts 2:42).
2. They Were Ever Eager to Receive the Word (Acts 8:4, 8).
3. They Were Depending upon the Power of Prayer (Acts 12:5).
4. They Were Faithful in Their Worship (Acts 2:42).
5. They Were Gathering about the Lord's Table (Acts 20:7).
6. They Were Noted for Their Liberal Giving (Acts 2:44–45).
7. They Were Abounding in Love One for Another (Eph. 1:15).

C. C. Maple

"LIVE IT DOWN"

1 Peter 2:12

I. **The World's Treatment of Christians**
   A. Enmity
   B. Defamation
   C. Perversion of the truth
   D. Aggravation of circumstances

II. **The Behavior Recommended**
   A. Honesty
   B. Consistency
   C. Truthfulness
   D. Purity
   E. Fidelity
   F. Circumspection

III. **The Results that Will Obtain**
   A. God will be glorified
   B. His religion will be honored
   C. Men will be saved

Pulpit Germs

THE CHRISTIAN'S BUSY LIFE

Ephesians 6:18

1. Always ready to testify for the Lord (Rom. 10:9–10; 1 Peter 3:15).

2. Always in communion with the Father (Ps. 119:147; Luke 18:1).

3. Always grateful for God's blessings (Eph. 5:20; 1 Thess. 5:18).

4. Always rejoicing (Phil. 4:4; 1 Thess. 5:16).

5. Always patient and kind (Col. 4:6; 2 Tim. 1:13).

6. Always abounding in the work of the Lord (1 Cor. 15:58).

7. Always obedient and true (Phil. 2:12; Col. 3:12–13, 16).

A. B. Carrero

HOW TO STRENGTHEN GOD'S SERVANTS

Nehemiah 2:18

How are the hands of the Lord's servants strengthened for good work?

1. By the joy of the Lord (Ezra 6:22; Neh. 8:10).

2. By prayer (Neh. 6:9; Isa. 40:31).

3. By hearing that their enemies are afraid (Judges 7:10–11).

4. By friendship (1 Sam. 23:16).

5. By the generosity of others (Ezra 1:6).

6. By increasing in the knowledge of God (Dan. 11:32).

7. By refusing to fear (Zech. 8:13).

8. By hearing how the Lord has strengthened others (Neh. 2:18).

Elizabeth Edmunds

A GOOD SOLDIER OF JESUS CHRIST

2 Timothy 2

I. He Must Be Strong (v. 1).
A. Strong in faith.
B. Strong in grace.
C. Strong in prayer.
D. Strong in determination (see Dan. 1:8).

II. He Must Be Able to Instruct Others (v. 2).
A. Able to train others for the ministry.
B. Able to ordain others for the ministry.
C. Able to be watchful and see that he ordains "faithful" men to the ministry.
D. Able to ordain men who will sincerely aim at the glory of God, honor of Christ, welfare of souls, and the advancement of the kingdom of God.

III. He Must Be Able to Endure Hardness (v. 3).
A. Soldier (v. 3).
B. Athlete (v. 5).
C. Husbandman (v. 6). The husbandman has to extract bread from the unwilling ground; and he may have to do this under unfavorable conditions.

IV. He Must Not Entangle Himself in the Affairs of This World (v. 4).
A. Business affairs.
B. Political affairs.
C. Social affairs (where immorality is involved).
D. The great care of a soldier should be to please his general. Jesus is our great general (see Heb. 2:9).

V. He Must See to It That in Carrying on Spiritual Warfare He Observes Laws of War (v. 5).
Study carefully Matthew 5:39–48; Romans 12:17–21; 2 Corinthians 10:4 for rules of warfare.

VI. He Must Be Willing to Wait for Rewards (v. 6).
A. If we would be partakers of fruits, we must labor.
B. If we would gain the prize, we must run the race.

C. If we would receive the promises, we must do the will of God (see Heb. 10:35–39).

VII. **He Must Be Able to Suffer (vv. 8–13).**
   A. Paul suffered as an evil doer (v. 9).
   B. Paul suffered cheerfully (v. 10).

VIII. **He Must Be a Student of the Word of God (vv. 14–26).**
   A. He must be able to edify others (v. 14).
   B. He must be able to rightly divide the word of truth (v. 15).
   C. He must be able to shun foolish questions (v.16).
   D. He must be able to name and expose heretics (vv. 17–21).
   E. He must be able to conquer his own lusts (vv. 22–23).
   F. He must be able to deliver sinners out of the snare of the Devil (vv. 24–26). See Luke 4:18; Acts 26:16–18.

Author Unknown

COMMON DELUSIONS

Proverbs 16:25

1. **Trusting in our own forefathers for salvation (Matt. 3:9).**

2. **That praying with many words is of value (Matt. 6:7–8).**

3. **That any foundation will do (Matt. 6:25, 27).**

4. **That we will have time tomorrow (Heb. 3:13; 4:7; James 4:13).**

5. **That men can argue with God (Matt. 7:21–23; Isa. 45:9).**

6. **That they can err with impunity (Heb. 3:9–11).**

7. **That riches are a great help (Ps. 49:6–8; Luke 12:19–20).**

8. **That any religion can be just as good (John 14:6; Acts 4:12).**

C. C. Maple

CHRIST PREACHED FROM PETER'S BOAT

Luke 5:1–11

I. The Consecration of the Boat (v. 3)
As He used the boat so He can use us (Rom. 1:14–16; 12:1–2; Isa. 6:8). To the degree that we consecrate we shall reap.

II. The Command to Launch Out (v. 4)
When Christ takes possession, He commissions for service (Matt. 28:19–20; Acts 26:16–17).
If we would catch—
A. Launch out.
B. Let down nets.

III. The Confession of Human Failure (v. 5)
Much toil and activity results in nothing (Matt. 7:21–22). Is it *our* plan or His that we follow? (see 1 Corinthians 12:7–9). He knows my way.

IV. The Confidence in Christ's Word (v. 5)
Faith is the way to victory (Acts 8:26; 13:2; 16:9). Danger of depending upon feelings when it is faith (Rom. 10:17).

V. The Conclusion of the Story (vv. 6–11)
Full nets—Christ's power again. In seeing Christ Peter saw himself. Discipleship (vv. 11, 27–28; 9:23). "I will make you fishers of men" (see also 1 Chron. 29:5; Mark 10:17–27).

C. C. Maple

OUR HOPE

The Coming of the Lord for His Church is—
A. A saving hope—(Rom. 8:24).
B. A good hope—(2 Thess. 2:16).
C. A blessed hope—(Titus 2:13).
D. A joyful hope—(Heb. 3:6).
E. A living hope—(1 Peter 1:3).
F. A purifying hope—(1 John 3:3).
G. A hope of righteousness—(Gal. 5:5).

Twelve Baskets Full

SERVICE OF THE BELIEVER

There are many illustrations we find which bring out the character of those who serve. There is the service of—

1. **The Priest** in the Temple (Heb. 9:11–14).
2. **The Slave** in the House (Luke 17:8).
3. **The Deacon** in the Church (Luke 22:26).
4. **The Elder** in the Flock (Rom. 1:9).
5. **The Son** in the Family (Matt. 4:10).
6. **The Maid** in the Home (Acts 12:13).
7. **The Member** in the Body (1 Cor. 12:21).

F. E. Marsh

PRACTICAL CHRISTIANITY

James 1:22

1. **Comfort one another (1 Thess. 5:11; 1 Peter 3:8).**
2. **Forbear with one another (Eph. 4:2, 32).**
3. **Forgive one another (Eph. 4:32; Col. 3:13).**
4. **Pray for one another (Deut. 9:20; James 5:16).**
5. **Edify one another (Rom. 14:19; Heb. 3:13).**
6. **Minister to one another (Gal. 5:13; 1 Peter 4:10).**
7. **Have peace one with another (Mark 9:50; 1 John 1:7).**

A. B. Carrero

SOME GREAT BIBLE PROPOSITIONS

2 Corinthians 4:18

1. We are poor, yet make many rich (2 Cor. 6:10).

2. We have victory, when we are defeated (2 Cor. 12:7–10).

3. We are great, when we become little (Matt. 18:4).

4. We enjoy rest, when we take the yoke (Matt. 11:29).

5. We save our life, when we lose it (Matt. 10:39; Luke 9:24).

6. We are free, when we become servants (Rom. 6:22).

7. We know we live, when we are dead (Rom. 6:6–8; Gal. 2:20).

A. B. Carrero

THE GENTLE SERVANT

2 Timothy 2:24

I. **The Example of Gentleness**
   A. Enjoined upon servants by Paul (2 Cor. 10:1a).
   B. Found only in Christ (2 Cor. 10:1b).

II. **The Display of Gentleness**
   A. As a nurse in the care of children (1 Thess. 2:7).
   B. As when leading those with young (Isa. 40:11).
   C. As love manifests its longings (1 Thess. 2:8).

III. **The Proof of Gentleness**
   A. Utter lack of covetousness (Acts 20:33).
   B. Unaffected affection (Acts 20:36–37).
   C. Tenderness of heart (Phil. 3:18).

S. F. Logsdon

MINISTERIAL JOY

1 Thessalonians 2:20

Introduction

It is a blessed thing for members of Christian churches when sincere and faithful ministers think well of them; when they can say, like Paul, "That I may be comforted together with you by the mutual faith both of you and me" (Rom. 1:12).

I. The Characters Who Are the Joy of Faithful Ministers

It is not the mere hearers of the word—not the merely professional—not formalists—or the lukewarm, or apathetic.

A. Those who have been converted by ministerial labor.

B. Those who enjoy salvation by faith in the sacrifice of Christ.

C. Those who cordially believe the Gospel—from the heart, and maintain an inviolable attachment to it in times of opposition.

D. Those who maintain the Christian character before the world.

E. Those who make progress in spirituality, and are becoming rich in Christian experience.

F. Those who abound in charity or love.

II. Why Such Characters Inspire Ministers with Joy

If the minister be a mere hireling, who does not seek you, but yours, he will not be much concerned about your spiritual state, but if he is the Lord's servant, watching for souls, etc., it will be the life of his soul. Hence Paul said, "For now" (1 Thess. 3:8). "For ye are our glory and joy."

A. The existence of such characters affords an evidence of ministerial fidelity—that they have not handled the Word of God deceitfully.

B. It is an answer to prayer—probably prayers mingled with tears. "They who sow in tears shall reap in joy."

C. In them the great object of the Christian ministry is answered—conversion of sinners.

D. It glorifies Christ. He sees of the travail of his soul. The minister is anxious to honor Him in the salvation of man.

E. The conversion and salvation of sinners will give efficiency to the church in advancing the kingdom of Christ.

F. Faithful ministers rejoice on the ground of mutual recognition in heaven. We are not merely companions on earth. We shall associate in glory.

Application

Does the church, do ministers, regard me now with joy, or with grief?

Our conduct here will influence eternity.

How terrible will be the state of those who are not benefited by ministerial labor!

Author Unknown

SEVEN FACTS ABOUT THE PEOPLE OF GOD

1 Peter 2:9–12

1. **They Are a Saved People** (Acts 2:47).
   The Lord adds only saved people to His Church (Titus 2:11–14).

2. **They Are a Free People** (John 8:36).
   Before Christ came—bondage of sin and law (Rom. 6:17–18; Gal. 5:1).

3. **They Are a Secure People** (1 Peter 1:5).
   His power is mighty—it saves and it keeps (John 10:27–29; Jude 24).

4. **They Are a Redeemed People** (Isa. 43:1).
   Redeemed by Blood—ransomed—purchased—liberated (Heb. 9:12; 1 John 4:18–19).

5. **They Are a Peculiar People** (Titus 2:14).
   Not "odd" folk. The Lord's exclusive people (Deut. 14:2; 1 Peter 2:9).

6. **They Are the Body of Christ** (Eph. 3:6).
   Christ is the Head, individuals are the members (John 15:5; Eph. 4:4–6).

7. **They Are to Be with Christ in Glory** (John 17:24).
   The Church called out for a future work (Eph. 2:4–7; Rev. 3:21; 5:10).

C. C. Maple

LABORERS TOGETHER WITH GOD

1 Corinthians 3:9

Introduction

It is necessary that we realize the importance of labor if we expect to succeed in serving the Lord.

Our choice of service must be legitimate.

It should offer a challenge.

It should have a fair promise of reward.

Our text tells us that we are laborers together with God.

I. We Are Laborers

A. Work is a privilege.

B. All worthwhile accomplishments are completed through constructive work.

II. We Are Laborers Together

A. It is important that we learn to cooperate and work together. Many of the world's troubles today are caused by failure to learn this truth.

B. We must find a way, and we can, to work together.

C. Cooperation in the cause of God is important. Each of us has his place. Some have talents and gifts others do not have.

III. We Are Laborers Together with God

A. We are yokemates with God.

B. We are dependent upon God.

C. God helps in a big way.

Illustration

A retired minister planted his garden in the spring, but when plants began to grow no rains came. He kept his garden barely alive with a long-neck two-gallon sprinkler and pumping water from the well. Even then they seemed to be withering away and dying. One morning a cloud appeared, rain came, watered his garden and his neighbors'. Although he could hardly keep a small garden alive with his best efforts, God could send a rain and make gardens and fields and pastures grow abundantly.

Conclusion

We can do a little by ourselves. We can do much more working together in the church with God and our fellows.

D. M. Duke

SERVICE

I. Qualifications for Service
   A. *Choice.* "Few chosen" (Matt. 20:16).
   B. *Preparation.* "Prepared unto every good work" (2 Tim. 2:2l).
   C. *Fitness.* "Meet for the master's use" (2 Tim. 2:21).
   D. *Obedience.* "He repented, and went" (Matt. 21:29).
   E. *Unity.* "Ourselves together" (Ezra 4:3).

II. Results
   A. *Success.* "The foundation . . . was laid" (Ezra 3:12).
   B. *Joy.* "To praise the Lord" (Ezra 3:10).
   C. *God glorified.* "They glorified God in me" (Gal. 1:24).

Author Unknown

SOME AIMS OF RIGHTEOUS LIVING

Psalm 39:1

As we as members and friends begin this ministry in this place, let us jointly decide:

1. **I will praise the Lord (Ps. 89:1).**
2. **I will love to go to church (Ps. 27:4; Heb. 10:25).**
3. **I will love my people (Rom. 12:10; 2 Thess. 3:13).**
4. **I will study my Bible (2 Tim. 2:15; 2 Peter 1:19).**
5. **I will bring my offerings to the Lord (Mal. 3:10).**
6. **I will use kind words (Prov. 15:1; 1 Cor. 13:7).**
7. **I will pray more often (Mark 14:38; Luke 18:1).**

A. B. Carrero

John Eliot, on the day of his death, in his eightieth year, was found teaching the alphabet to an Indian child at his bedside. "Why not rest from your labors?" asked a friend.

"Because," said the venerable man, "I have prayed to God to make me useful to the close of my earthly pilgrimage, and He has heard my prayer. Now that I can no longer preach, He leaves me strength enough to teach this poor child his alphabet."

CHRISTIAN LIVING

Romans 6:4

As this work for God is launched to His glory and by His grace, let us corporately decide that we will:

1. **Walk not after the flesh (Rom. 8:1; Gal. 5:16).**

2. **Walk by faith (2 Cor. 5:7; Heb. 11:33–34).**

3. **"Walk worthy of the Lord" (Eph. 4:1; 5:8; Col. 1:10).**

4. **Walk not as fools (Eph. 5:15; Col. 4:5).**

5. **Walk honestly (Rom. 13:13; 1 Thess 4:12).**

6. **Walk in all sincerity (Eph. 4:17–25; 5:8).**

7. **Live a consecrated life (Rom. 8:13; Gal. 5:24; Titus 2:12).**

A. B. Carrero

SOME MEN OF GOD

Jeremiah 35:15

The Old Testament is full of illustrations of godly men whose lives made a difference. Consider:

1. **Reformation in the days of King Asa (1 Kings 15:22).**

2. **Reformation in the days of Josiah (2 Kings 23:24).**

3. **Reformation in the days of Hezekiah (2 Chron. 31:1).**

4. **Reformation and revival in Ezra's time (Ezra 10:3).**

5. **Reformation and revival in Nehemiah's time (Neh. 13:19ff).**

6. **Men of God in olden times (Abraham) (Gen. 12:1).**

7. **Moses and Aaron leaders of the people (Ex. 3:10; 28:1; Deut. 33:1).**

Author Unknown

VISIONS AND VOICES

Acts 26:19

Introduction

Early on the morning of August 3, 1492, three vessels sailed from Palos, Spain; on October 12, 1492, they glided into the harbor of a new world. Columbus saw a vision and heard a voice.

I. **God Selects Prepared Agents for Great Tasks**
   A. Moses prepared to deliver Israel.
   B. Ezekiel prepared to interpret oriental symbolism.
   C. Isaiah prepared to become an evangelical prophet.
   D. Paul prepared to become a missionary to Gentiles.

II. **God Gives a Vision of Himself for Great Tasks**
   A. To Moses, He was omnipotent—a wonder-working God.
   B. To Ezekiel, He was immanent—an ever-present God.
   C. To Isaiah, He was eminent—a high and holy God.
   D. To Paul, He was permanent—a never-changing God.

III. **God Speaks with a Certain Voice for Great Tasks**
   A. What did His servants hear?
      1. A call to personal purity.
      2. A call to personal service.
      3. A call to personal witness.
   B. Christians today need to hear His voice in personal calling.

E. S. Phillips

HOW WE COME TO BE CHRISTIANS

Galatians 3:26

1. Chosen in Christ (Eph. 1:4; James 2:5).

2. Freed from condemnation (John 5:24; Rom. 8:1).

3. Created in Christ (Eph. 2:10; Titus 2:7, 14; 3:8).

4. Conformed to the image of Christ (Rom. 8:29; 1 John 3:3).

5. Living for Him (Gal. 2:20; Col. 3:8–16).

6. Complete in Him (Eph. 4:13; Col. 2:10).

7. Safe in His keeping (2 Tim. 1:12; 1 Peter 1:5).

A. B. Carrero

CHRISTIAN LAW AND ORDER

Ephesians 5:21

In the Bible the word "submit" has the idea of "adjusting to" as well as "surrendering to." That applies to all of life, not just the wedding relationship.

1. Wives submit to your husbands (Eph. 5:22; Col. 3:18).

2. Children submit to discipline (Prov. 29:17; Heb. 12:9).

3. Submit to your pastors (1 Thess. 5:12–13; Heb. 13:17).

4. Submit to human government (Rom. 13:1; 1 Peter 2:13).

5. Young people submit to your elders (1 Peter 5:5).

6. Submit yourselves to God (Rom. 6:13; James 4:7).

7. Submit to the Divine will of God (Matt. 6:10; 26:39).

A. B. Carrero

WEDDING GUESTS AND GARMENTS

Matthew 22:1–14

Introduction

We believe this parable has a definite application to the future kingdom to be established by our Lord, personally, at the time of His return. We also believe it illustrates principles which are now in operation as the Holy Spirit chooses and calls out a people who shall constitute and comprise the body and bride of the heavenly Bridegroom. It also has some bearing on the marriage relationship. Read the parable thoughtfully several times in the light of its context and setting.

Let us closely observe seven outstanding aspects of the parable as it applies to the present:

I.   **Suitable Comparison** (See Rom. 7:2–4).

The marriage feast with all its provision and pleasure is a practical illustration of what God has provided in the Gospel: redemption, the new birth, pardon, life, peace, joy, grace, power, heaven, etc.

II.   **The Son the Central Figure**—"For His Son" (see Col. 1:18).

III.   **The Completeness of It All**—"All things *are* Ready."

IV.   **The Costliness of It**—"Oxen and fatlings killed." The gospel feast called for the slaughter of a special Lamb (see John 1:29, 36; 1 Peter 1:18–19; Rev. 5:6, 12).

V.   **The Call to the Feast**—"Come unto the marriage feast."

The king calls, invites, through his servants. So it is with God. There are two calls here. The first was to the Jews of Jesus' day. They refused, and suffered fearful retribution as history shows (see vv. 5–7.) The second call is international and universal. "To every creature" (Mark 16:15–16; see also vv. 8–10; Acts 15:13–17). Church history, and the present, proves the truth of these statements.

VI.   **The Conditions to Be Met**

A. Relish for the food. The Jews had none (see v. 5).

B. Relish and regard for other guests. The Jews had neither.

C. Reception of the invitation (see vv. 8, 10; 21:43).

D. The robe required as a fitness for His presence (see Isa. 61:10).

VII. The Consequences

A. "The wedding furnished with guests." Our Lord will have a bride and a queen.

B. The King *came* in to see and to scrutinize.

C. The unclothed professor with a closed mouth cast out (vv. 11–13).

Conclusion

"Jesus, thy blood and righteousness, My only dress, my beauty is; With these in flaming worlds arrayed, With joy shall I lift up my head."

John A. Ross

CHRISTIAN GIVING

Luke 6:38

I. **The Whole Basis of Christianity Rests upon This One Word—***Give*
   A. God gave His Son (John 3:16)
   B. Jesus gave Himself (Gal. 2:20)
   C. We should imitate God and give, as He gave—
      1. Ourselves (2 Cor. 8:5)
      2. Our substance (Prov. 3:9–10)

II. **How We Are to Give**
   A. Out of a perfect heart (1 Chron. 29:9)
   B. Willingly (2 Cor. 9:7)
   C. Abundantly (Luke 6:38)

III. **Some Who Gave of Their Substance to the Lord, and Were Blessed Thereby—**
   A. Abraham (Heb. 7:1–2)
   B. The woman who was a sinner (Luke 7:37)
   C. The poor widow (Luke 21:1, 4)

IV. **As We Give to God and His Cause, So We May Expect He Will Give to Us**
   (Luke 6:38; Prov. 11:24)

Author Unknown

A young Indian convert once brought Bishop Whipple a two-dollar bill which he requested him to change, that he and his wife might each give half to the Lord's work. "Is this all the money you have?" asked the bishop. The man replied that it was.

The bishop was about to remonstrate and advise him to give part of it, when another saved Indian whispered in his ear: "It might be too much for a white man to give, but not too much for a poor Indian, who has this year for the first time heard of his Savior." What a rebuke this is to the lukewarm Christians who live on the fatness of the good land God has given them, and seem to feel no responsibility to give of their abundance to the work of carrying the Gospel to others!

Selected

THE CHRISTIAN AND HIS MONEY

2 Corinthians 9:7

1. **Everything we have belongs to God (Ps. 50:10–12).**

2. **When we give, we pay a debt (Mal. 3:8–10).**

3. **When we give, we make a treasure in heaven (Luke 12:33).**

4. **Even the poor can give and God sees it (Mark 12:42–44).**

5. **Be faithful in our offerings (1 Cor. 16:2).**

6. **Help others with our means (Acts 9:36–39; 11:29).**

7. **Honor God with our gifts (Prov. 3:9).**

A. B. Carrero

GIVING TO THE LORD

Exodus 35–36; Acts 20:35

Notice

I. **The Universality of Their Giving**
   A. "And Moses gathered all . . ."
   B. It had been all receiving up to this point.

II. **The Variety and Extent of the Giving**
   A. The work of their hands and the fruit of their labors.
   B. The gratitude of their hearts.

III. **The Manner and Spirit of Their Giving**
   A. Promptly.
   B. Willingly and heartily.
   C. Self-denyingly.
   D. Because they were a forgiven and a redeemed people.

Conclusion

Cite the words of Paul to the Corinthians. "Ye know the grace of our Lord Jesus Christ that, though he was rich, yet for our sakes he became poor, that we through his poverty might be made rich."

J. H. W.

INVESTMENTS

Matthew 19:27–30

Introduction

Many people today are defeated spiritually because their motive for following Jesus is wrong. He came to rule men through their hearts rather than by force. Many followed Him while miracles were being performed but fled at Calvary. We have many miracle followers today, but the crowd that follows Him to Calvary is comparatively small. We will either follow Him out of gratitude and place our all at His feet, or like Peter, follow Him for what we can get out of it. Greatest dividends of the future will be those from investments in the kingdom of God.

I. **Our Life Is the Greatest Investment We Can Make** (Matt. 10:39).
   A. This investment has two divisions:
      1. What we *must* do. Right relationship toward God and man.
      2. What we *may* do. Go beyond duty and obligations. In an old issue of the *Saturday Evening Post*, Whittaker Chambers said, "The death of religious faith is in nothing so much as in the fact that, in general, it has lost its power to move anyone to die for it."
   B. We should be willing to invest our all because of our influence on others. It is said that Nero had to quit persecuting the early Christians because too many were being converted to Christianity through their joy in dying for Him.

II. **Our Next Investment Should Be Our Means**
   A. A tithe is really not ours to invest, but just as sure as we pay it the Lord will bless (Mal. 3:10).
   B. Offerings. The Scripture states, "Tithes *and* offerings."

III. **Examples of Being Owned of God:**
   A. Paul counted all "but dung" that he might follow Christ.
   B. A lady in Oklahoma gave her money saved for a car that the doors of the church might remain open when it looked as if they would be closed because of lack of money.

C. It is said Dr. and Mrs. H. F. Reynolds gave their savings that missionaries could remain on the field.

D. A man in Hugo, Oklahoma, mortgaged his home that the church might be rebuilt after being burned to the ground.

IV. Results of Investing All Are Worthwhile

A. Revivals in the church. Dr. Chapman used to say that a liberal church was a spiritual church.

B. We save ourselves by investing in others. The king of England was once ready to make one of his yearly broadcasts to his kingdom when a broken wire was discovered. An attendant of the station took both ends of the broken wire in his hands, thus completing a circuit. The message was given. God wants to get the message of peace to a lost and dying world.

L. I. Weaver

UNBOUNDING LIBERALITY

Romans 15:25–27

1. **Give Gratefully (Rom. 15:27).**

2. **Give Methodically (1 Cor. 16:2).**

3. **Give Cheerfully (2 Cor. 9:7).**

4. **Give Abundantly (2 Cor. 8:7).**

5. **Give All (2 Cor. 8:2).**

R. Lee

Law of the Garden

To a friend who protested against receiving a large quantity of flowers, the owner of the garden replied, "I shall not rob myself, for it is the constant cutting of the flowers that makes them grow so luxuriously." The more we give away, the more we have to give.

Christian Herald

GIVING AND GETTING

Acts 20:35

Introduction

Does one's interest in religion lie with what he can give or what he can get?

I. The Getter Is a Lopsided Christian

A. He comes to church to enjoy himself, demanding a certain atmosphere. He decides whether he likes the preacher and the preaching.

B. He insists that people treat him just so. He requires a certain amount of praise and handshaking.

C. He longs for heaven, and sings, "O land of rest, for thee I sigh." Why do some who do so little get weary?

II. It Is Better to Give Than to Get

A. You find that, as you give out of the fullness of your heart, God replenishes and overflows you.

B. Examples: at Cana the wine vessels were refilled. The widow's oil continued to flow as it was used. The manna was good only when used.

C. There are distinguishing marks of one who is determined to be a giver:

1. He comes to church to contribute, to enrich the lives of others. His songs, his words, his spirit, his face—all contribute something.
2. He demands nothing in return for his help.
3. His thought is not how people treat him but how he treats them. He will support any reasonable idea. He boosts every preacher, receives every message.
4. He regards religion, not as something to enjoy, but to use. He is ready at every call for volunteers. He responds to every financial need.

III. The Giver Is Happier Than the Getter

A. He knows happiness is not found by seeking it, but by losing self in service.

B. Through accepting Christ, receiving the Holy Spirit, obeying the Word, he serves and gives out of the fullness of his heart.

C. Giving all is the secret of happiness.

Conclusion
Perhaps you cannot be a giver because you have not enough of grace for yourself. You may be spiritually empty. Let God fill your life, then find your highest happiness in giving.

adapted from *Donald H. Strong*

PERSONAL RESPONSIBILITY

Matthew 25:15

Introduction
In every parable Jesus sought to teach a central truth. Lost sheep, coin, son—truth of individual worth. Flowers of the field—truth of individual care. In this parable He taught truth of individual responsibility.

I. Notice The Distribution of Talents.
A. Each man received according to individual ability.

B. Each man received his amount for the same purpose.

C. Each man received something to use in furthering the Master's business.

II. Notice the Treatment of Talents.
A. Each man was tempted.
1. The five-talent man (exceptional man) determined not to get by with less than his best.
2. The two-talent man (average man) decided to slide by with the crowd.
3. The one-talent man (limited man) excused himself because of his lack of ability.

B. Two men would not yield to temptation—they succeeded.

C. The third man yielded to temptation—he failed.

III. Notice the Day of Reckoning.
A. Judgment was not on basis of returns but on faithfulness.

B. The Master's disposition of us is based on our disposition of Him and His work here.

E. S. Phillips

BLESSINGS OF GIVING

Acts 20:35

Introduction

Paul quotes the words of Jesus. Human nature says, "No, it can't be true." The spirit and practice of the world say no, but the Spirit of Christ in His own people answers yes.

I. That Which Makes It Possible and Real

A. Jesus sets the example.

B. His salvation destroys the spirit of the world.

C. His grace infuses the divine into human nature, making self-sacrifice a real pleasure.

II. Can Be Our Experience and Practice

A. It is possible to reach a place where one can be more blessed in giving out than in receiving.

B. We must get where we delight in doing good.

C. The widow gave her all with pleasure (Mark 12:41). The early church set us a wonderful example (Acts 4:32–37).

III. Reason Why It Is True

A. No true and lasting happiness comes from selfish gratification.

    1. Real happiness comes from sacrificing for others.

    2. What we give is saved. What we spend on ourselves is lost (John 6:27).

    3. Instruction to the rich (6:6–11, 17–19).

B. The motive back of our giving rates the measure of blessedness and happiness we derive from it.

    1. Love must be the motive (2 Cor. 8:1–8).

    2. Cain and Abel (Gen. 4:3–4); Jacob (Gen. 28:22); (Prov. 19:17); (1 Cor. 9:14).

IV. Some of the Benefits Received from Giving

A. Spirituality in the giver (2 Cor. 9:6–12).

B. It increases both spirituality and temporal prosperity (Prov. 3:9–10; 11:24–25; Phil. 4:15–19).

C. How God rewards (Luke 6:38).

D. It pleases God (Heb. 13:16).

Harold E. Priddy

THE TITHE FOR THE LORD

Malachi 3:10

Introduction

These are the words of the Lord to His people. The truths of the Bible about tithing are found in this passage.

1. The Lord's People and the Tithe

"Bring ye." All people who are true children of God should rejoice to honor the Lord and His kingdom with at least a tithe of their income. Every Christian should follow the teaching of the Bible and give one-tenth of his earnings to the Lord. It belongs to God. All Christians should give all the tithe for all the work of the Lord.

2. The Lord's Plea for the Tithe

"Bring ye all the tithes." This is the word of the Lord. It is the voice of God. This is the command of the Word of God. It is the teaching of the entire Bible.

3. The Lord's Place for the Tithe

"Into the storehouse." The Lord is clear in His teachings as to the place for His tithe. It is to be brought into His storehouse, into His treasury.

4. The Lord's Purpose of the Tithe

"That there may be meat in mine house." The Lord's money must care for the Lord's work. The tithe of all members of the church placed in the treasury of the church will provide ample funds for paying all bills, and promoting all missionary, educational, and benevolent work of the church. Keep the church property in best condition and all causes supported. This is the purpose of the tithe.

5. The Lord's Promise to the Tither

I will "open you the windows of heaven, and pour you out a blessing, that there shall not be room enough to receive it." The Lord will bless the tither. He will honor those who honor Him. Try the Lord. Put Him to the test. The Lord will always bless those who honor His house.

J. O. Williams

THE GRACE OF GIVING

2 Corinthians 8:7

Introduction

In the eighth and ninth chapters of this second Corinthian letter, Paul discourses on the grace of giving. The immediate need that prompted the discussion is the support for the poor Christians in Jerusalem. The basis on which he makes the appeal is sound for today. The appeal for a gift is based on:

1. The Need of the Cause

No doubt the real condition of the saints in Jerusalem was stated. Their poverty was explained. Their need was presented. The facts were stated and the appeal made. If Christians today could see the condition and need, their gifts would be more gracious.

2. The Liberality of Others

Paul appeals to the Christians of Corinth on the basis of what the members of the churches of Macedonia had done and the liberal gifts they had made. Out of their great trial of affliction and deep poverty, they had given to the full limit of their ability, and even beyond this, and even prayed the committee to accept the gifts. It often inspires many to give when they know the liberality of others in poorer circumstances. Jesus taught that the liberality of a gift must be judged not by the amount given, but by what was left when the gift was made. Paul emphasized this same doctrine (2 Cor. 8:12–16).

3. For the Sake of Consistency

Paul calls attention to the members of the church at Corinth that they were strict about other doctrines, and did "abound in everything, in faith, and utterance and knowledge, and in all diligence, and in your love to us" (2 Cor. 8:7). It would be inconsistent to abound in these and not in the grace of giving.

4. The Love of Christ

Paul calls upon Christians to remember the love of the Lord Jesus Christ who was abundantly rich but became poor that they through His poverty might be rich (2 Cor. 8:9). The love that Christ has for His people and what He has done, is doing and will do for them should stir their hearts to loyalty and to the most devoted activity for Him.

5. The Preservation of Self-Respect

Paul tells the Christians of Corinth that they were willing a year previously to make a gift, and had even made pledges. But he reminded them that the pledges were not paid and that he did not desire to be embarrassed or to embarrass them by not finding the pledges paid. He called on them: "Now therefore perform the doing of it" (v. 11).

6. The Approval of the Lord

Paul is clear in verses six to eleven of this ninth chapter of Corinthians that liberal giving from a heart of love will merit the love of the Lord and rich blessings from Him.

Accept the appeal that is here made. Practice liberal giving out of love for the Lord. Preach it to others until they will abound in the joy that comes from the practice of the grace of giving.

J. O. Williams

FUNDAMENTALS OF STEWARDSHIP

1 Corinthians 4:2

Introduction

The Gospel deals with all that a man is—body, soul and spirit—his person (1 Thess. 5:23).

The Gospel also deals with all that a man has—his possessions. This involves stewardship.

In the matter of stewardship are some fundamentals which all of us should know well.

I. Ownership. God Owns All.

A. Creation (Gen. 1:1; Ps. 24:1; Ezek. 18:4).
B. Preservation (Dan. 5:23; Acts 17:24–28).
C. Redemption (Isa. 43:1; 1 Cor. 6:19; 1 Peter 1:19–20).
D. Consecration. We are His by our own free will.

II. Stewardship. Man Is a Steward.

A steward is defined as one who is entrusted with the goods or property of another; thus one who manages or oversees for another or others.

A. Of person—me.
B. Of possessions—mine.
  1. Acquisition.
      a. John Wesley in a sermon on money said, "Make all you can; save all you can; give all you can."
      b. The Christian is responsible for securing the best possible for the body, mind and spirit.
      c. The Christian is to acquire honestly within the limits of the Ten Commandments, 1 Corinthians 13, and the Sermon on the Mount.
  2. Conservation.
      a. Wastefulness is sin.
      b. Seek the golden mean between being a spend-all or a miser.
  3. Distribution.
      a. Time.
      b. Talents.
      c. Money and goods.

III. Accounting. We Must Give Account of Our Stewardship.
A. Certainty. The fact of our giving account is sure.
B. Basis.
  1. Not according to the amount entrusted.
  2. Not according to the amount gained.
  3. According to faithfulness.
C. Results.
  1. Commendation—where faithful.
  2. Condemnation—where unfaithful.
  3. Compensation—reward or punishment.

Conclusion
May our commendation be: "Well done, good and faithful servant" (Matt. 25:23).

B. W. Downing

A THANKSGIVING MESSAGE

Philippians 4:7

I. Cheer Up
"Rejoice."
A. The duty: Rejoice; a calm, deep settled gladness in the soul.
B. The sphere: "in the Lord."
    1. In His atonement (Rom. 5:11).
    2. In His righteousness (Rom. 4).
    3. In His faithfulness (Phil. 1:6).
C. The time: "Always"; in sorrow, persecution, bereavement (Hab. 3:17–18). "Evermore" (1 Thess. 5:16).

II. Let Up
Be moderate—meaning yieldedness, giving way, forbearance, gentleness, patience.

III. Look Up
"The Lord is at hand."
A. Providentially (Ps. 139:1–10).
B. Spiritually. "Christ in you."
C. Personally. To punish evil and to care for His own.

IV. Cast Up
"Be careful for nothing." "Casting all your care upon Him" (1 Peter 5:7). God is able to take care of us and ours; able to make all grace abound, to make all things work together for our good.

V. Pray Up
Make your requests known, in everything by prayer and supplication.

VI. Praise Up
As blessings come down, praises should go up, and even before they come.

VII. Keep Up
This is only possible as we let the God of peace reign in our hearts. He, and He alone can keep us in perfect peace—can give us great peace.

Frederick Rader

MANIFEST REASONS FOR THANKSGIVING

Psalm 107:8

Introduction

It is noteworthy that the text is found four times in this psalm. It is truly Davidic to praise the Lord. We always speak highly of the truly eminent. God is infinitely excellent, sublime, holy, righteous and good. Witness His perfections.

I. Our Surroundings

A. We should truly thank God for our great and beloved nation.

    1. History of the Pilgrim fathers, Mayflower Compact, Constitution, Bill of Rights briefly told.

    2. Contrast with many other nations today.

B. We should thank God for the Christian home.

    1. God started the human race with a home.

    2. Its perpetuity depends upon its proper use.

    3. It should have a sacred place in our hearts and lives. Reading the Scriptures. Family worship. Christian conversation. Proper protection from vices.

II. Our Spiritual Heritage

A. We should heartily thank God for the blessed open Bible.

    1. Attitude of Russia, Spain, Communistic China—in contrast.

    2. We should prize it highly, use it frequently, follow its teachings, love its laws and precepts, abide by its principles and serve its Christ.

B. We should thank Almighty God for the church.

    1. "Upon this rock I will build my church, and the gates of hell shall not prevail against it."

    2. Infidelity, communism, liberals and all unbelievers cannot destroy it.

III. Our Salvation

A. We should thank God for the Cross.

    1. "When I survey the wondrous Cross."

    2. "God forbid that I should glory, save in the cross."

B. We should thank God for our future prospect—heaven.
   1. Trials, temptations, problems here below.
   2. A glorious release ere long.

Conclusion

We should thank God in everything and for everything.
"In everything give thanks" (1 Thess. 5:18).
"Giving thanks always for all things" (Eph. 5:20).

E. E. Wordsworth

THE REAL MEANING OF CHRISTMAS

Luke 2:20

Introduction

Christmas in many quarters has come to mean just another holiday, or another season for money-making. For some it is a time of worry about gifts to friends. Gifts, however, oftentimes obscure the real meaning of Christmas, which is:

1. **That God loves man: "Fear not" (v. 10; see also John 3:16).**

2. **That God's love is manifested: "For, Behold" (1 John 3:1).**

3. **That God showed His mercy before man sought it: "I bring" (Rom. 5:6–8).**

4. **That good tidings and joy are for every individual: "you" (Acts 13:32).**

5. **That God is no respecter of persons: "to all people" (Acts 10:34).**

6. **That salvation from sin is within reach of everyone (Isa. 52:10; Luke 2:11).**

7. **That God wants man to enjoy peace of heart, and good will among men (Luke 2:14).**

M. C. Marietta

THE VALUE OF THE RESURRECTION

1 Corinthians 15:17

1. Necessary to our salvation (Rom. 10:9–10).

2. Insures our justification (Rom. 4:25).

3. Gives us security (Rom. 8:34; Heb 7:25).

4. Produces fruitfulness (Rom. 7:4).

5. Energizes believers (Rom. 5:10; Gal. 2:20).

6. Assures of righteous judgment (Acts 17:31).

7. Guarantees our resurrection (John 14:19; 1 Cor. 15:20–23; 1 Thess. 4:13–18).

8. Certifies resurrection of all men (John 5:28–29; Acts 24:15; 1 Cor. 15:22).

Treasures of Bible Truth

Transformation

The cross was such an ugly thing!—
A shape to make the heart afraid;
A beam of death for lawless men,
A gibbett for the renegade.

The cross is such a lovely thing!—
The lamp in night where people grope;
The emblem of eternal life;

The symbol of eternal hope;
The subject of a thousand songs;
The sign of truth and liberty.

The cross was such an ugly thing
Until it went to Calvary.

Lon Woodrum